GEORGE WASHINGTON
STARTS A WAR

BRUCE R. KINDIG

Copyright © 2023 Bruce R. Kindig.

All rights reserved. No part of this book may be reproduced, stored, or transmitted by any means—whether auditory, graphic, mechanical, or electronic—without written permission of both publisher and author, except in the case of brief excerpts used in critical articles and reviews. Unauthorized reproduction of any part of this work is illegal and is punishable by law.

ISBN: 979-8-89031-676-9 (sc)
ISBN: 979-8-89031-677-6 (hc)
ISBN: 979-8-89031-678-3 (e)

Because of the dynamic nature of the Internet, any web addresses or links contained in this book may have changed since publication and may no longer be valid. The views expressed in this work are solely those of the author and do not necessarily reflect the views of the publisher, and the publisher hereby disclaims any responsibility for them.

One Galleria Blvd., Suite 1900, Metairie, LA 70001
(504) 702-6708

DEDICATION

This book is dedicated to all students of history. There are lessons of history that teach us things we should not repeat. Some are in this book.

CONTENTS

Introduction xi

Chapter 1 French and English in America 1

Chapter 2 Eighteenth Century Warfare 5

Chapter 3 George Washington and the Frontier 11

Chapter 4 The Albany Conference 16

Chapter 5 General Braddock and the Lessons of War 20

Chapter 6 The Acadians 25

Chapter 7 Undeclared War Continues 28

Chapter 8 French Victories 33

Chapter 9 The Grand Plan 37

Chapter 10 The Battle of Quebec 43

Chapter 11 Pontiac and the Treaty of Paris 48

Chapter 12 Epilogue and Biographies 52

Appendix 1: Fort Necessity Surrender Document 59

Appendix 2: Battle Chart 63

Annotated Bibliography 65

About the Author 69

NORTH AMERICA 1754

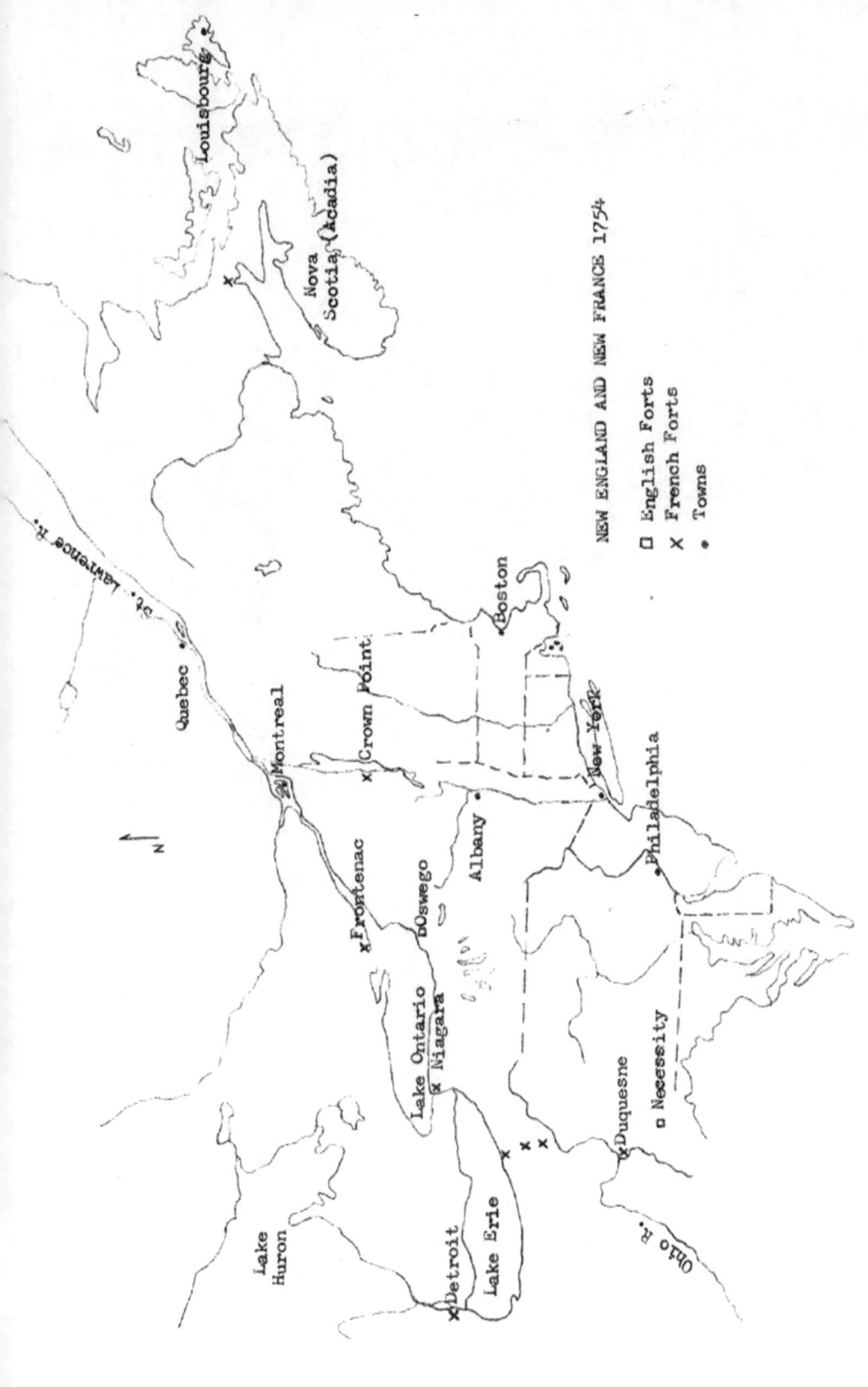

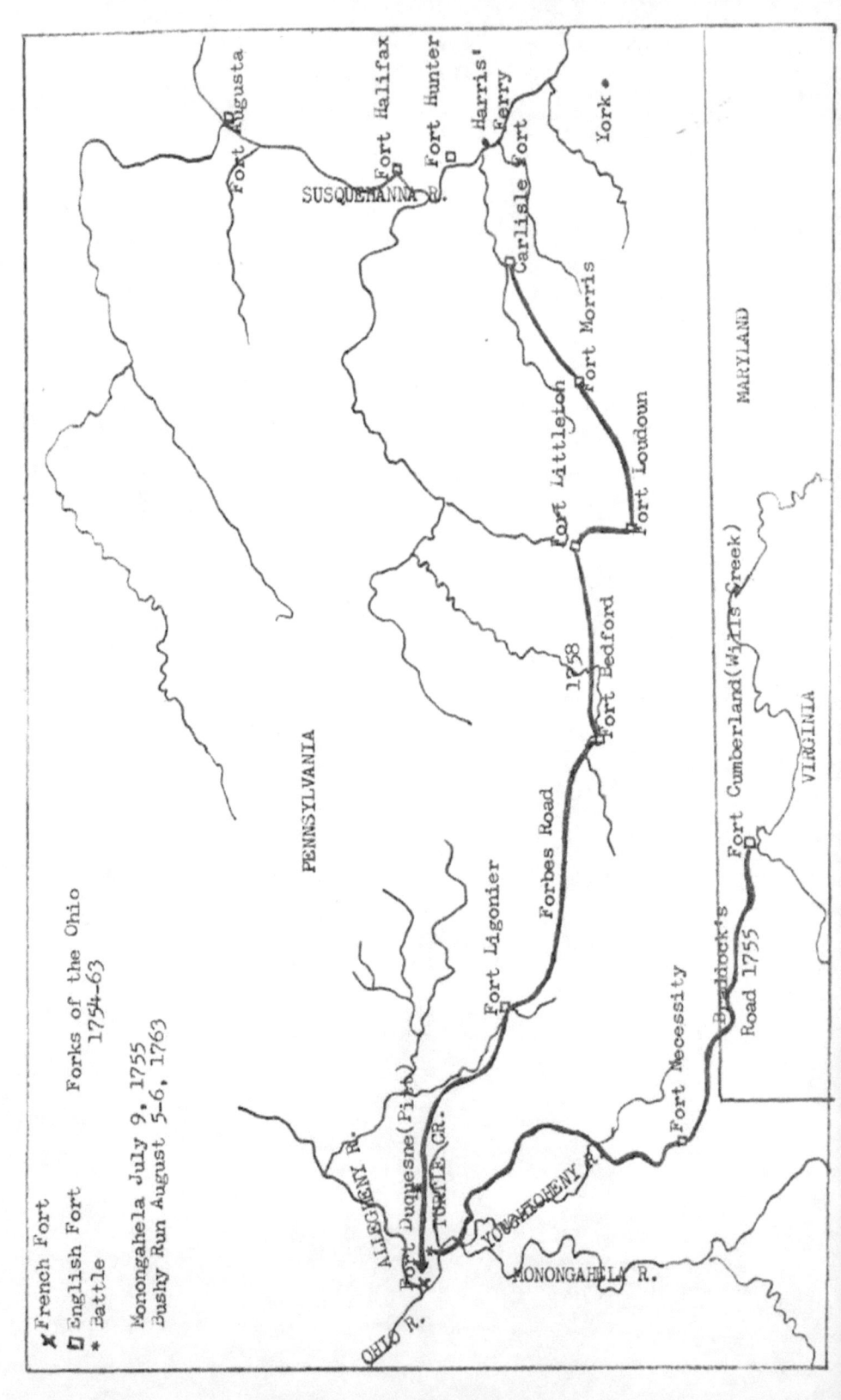

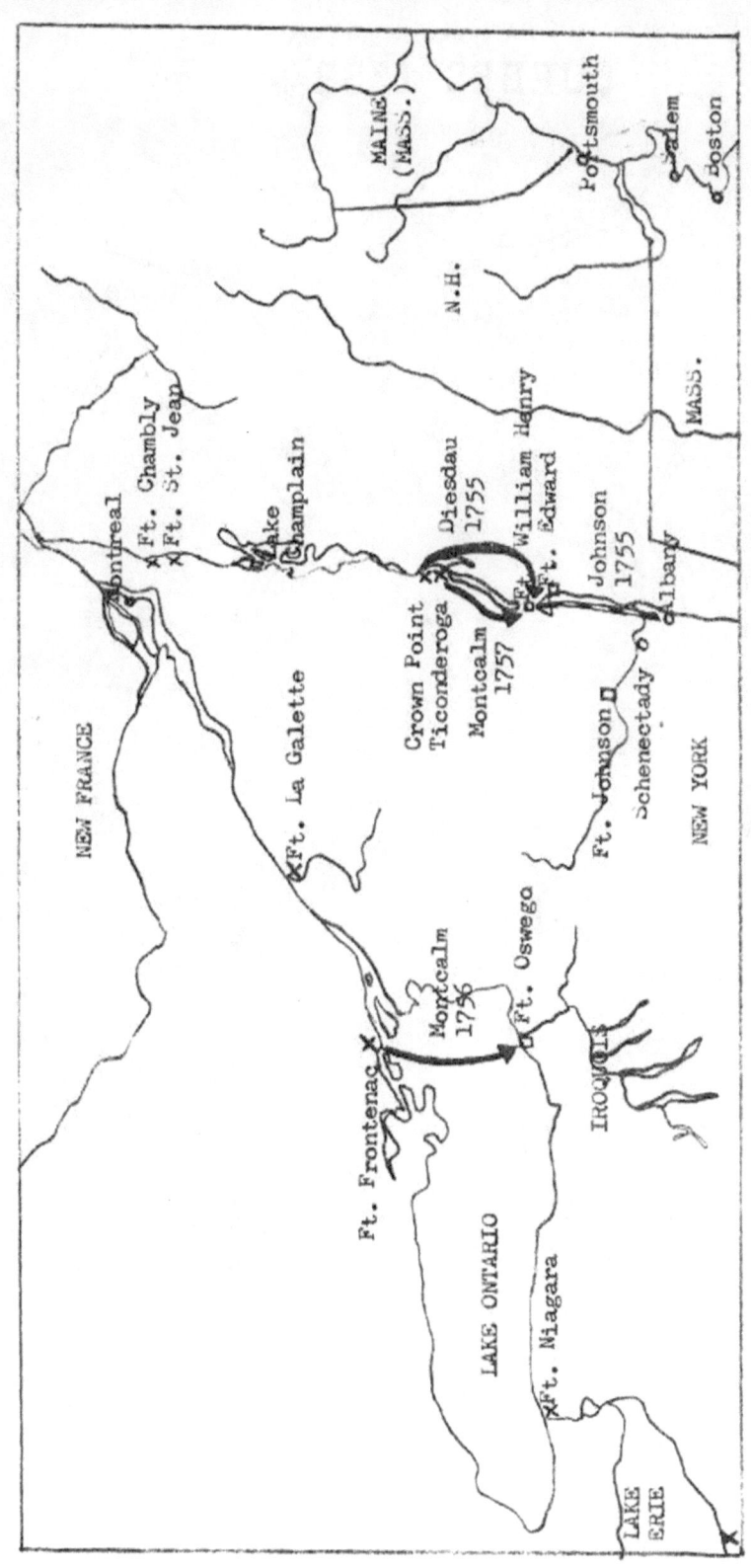

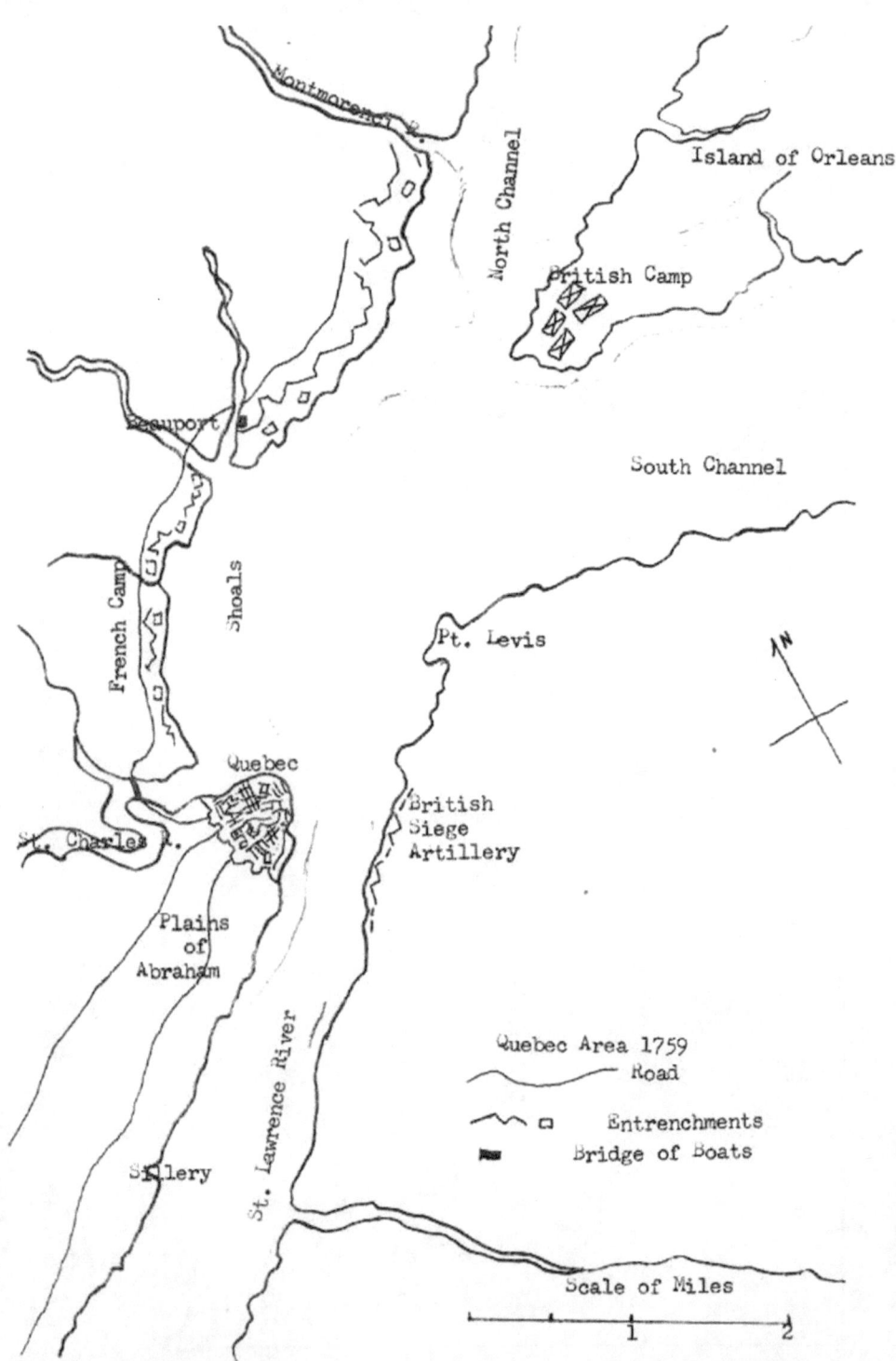

INTRODUCTION

When I originally wrote the manuscript for this book I intended it for a teenage audience who had very little background or knowledge of the events surrounding the French and Indian War. It dawned on me that many adults in the twenty-first century could also benefit to a nice introduction to a fascinating time period. So, I added some features but left the basics intact.

The focus will be on a young George Washington who had just taken over the Mount Vernon Plantation after the death of his half-brother, Lawrence Washington, in 1752. George will eventually be overcome by the many events going on around him and will slowly become a minor character in the events dominated by others. That he slowly disappears in the narrative is due to the overwhelming influence of people from Britain, but George Washington is definitely the one who started this war and admitted to it in writing.

Many people will be mentioned in this book and to help the reader to know more about them the last chapter will include a number of brief biographies. These biographies will point out those who have learned the lessons of history and those who were doomed to repeat the worst of life. That is the other feature of this book. The lessons to learn from history. To understand these lessons, one must have an open mind. Learn from the past to improve your own destiny.

This book will serve as an introduction to a very important event in history. The annotated bibliography may be of interest for those interested in further reading. While researching this book, I visited many of the sites mentioned. Some are unchanged after more than 250 years, like Jumonville Glenn. While others are under modern paved streets and buildings, like the battlefield at the Battle of Monongahela outside of Pittsburg, Pennsylvania. Many of the forts mentioned in the book can be seen today as they are kept up by state or national parks and they have very nice museums. I will particularly mention Ft. Ligonier, in Pennsylvania and Fortress Louisbourg on Cape Breton Island. The Canadian government has done a fabulous job recreating a good portion of this fortress with everything focused on the year 1744, including a soldier's meal. I stood on the Plains of Abraham but had a hard time focusing on French and British troops in its modern setting. Students of history should always take any opportunity to visit historical sites. Stand outside Ft. Necessity, shut your eyes and imagine Indians moving through the woods. Then open your eyes slowly.

I will use the term Indians in this book to describe the native Americans because that was the word used back in the 18th century. Most other terms and place names I will use the modern names. One more thing. The term English and British often mean the same thing. The first twelve colonies were founded by England but after 1707 England and Scotland merged their two countries into one called Great Britain or officially the United Kingdom of England, Scotland and Ireland. The colonists usually called themselves English while the home government was actually British. The term colonists will sometimes be substituted with the word Americans. Although the colonists were English they were more and more considering themselves as Americans particularly when British soldiers are considered as separate from colonial soldiers. A dislike for each other began during this period and a feeling of difference could be made.

CHAPTER 1

FRENCH AND ENGLISH IN AMERICA

In 1750 the North American continent was divided between Spain, France and Great Britain without regard to the original Indian societies. There were no boundaries between these European claims and each viewed the wealth of this continent differently. Spain saw wealth as gold and silver, France saw wealth in the fur trade and England saw wealth from commercial trade with her colonies. These contrasting views of wealth of the continent is the main reason for conflict between these nations. The English colonists wanted more land for expansion and the French wanted to prevent this expansion. The winner of this contest could increase its wealth and power.

The English first began colonies in America in 1607. Many people came to these colonies for the chance to own their own property, to earn a better living, for freedom of worship as they please or for the freedom to share in government. Some came to America to avoid military service in Europe. By 1750 there were thirteen English colonies with a population of about 1,500,000. These colonies were close together along the Atlantic coast and had a thriving trade with England.

The colonists near the coast soon built towns and established private business, some were part of a world trade network. The colonists further inland lived in a frontier area with Indians nearby. They cleared the land and built their own homes and farms. These activities led to a feeling of freedom and liberty.

The English colonies were more democratic and individualistic than England itself. As early as 1619 representative government had been established in Virginia and the Pilgrims had pledged fair and equal laws to everyone in 1620. English tradition had been brought to America and with the addition of the American environment the colonies produced a stronger democracy. The English colonists were hard working independent people. There were few wealthy people and the ability to move from being poor to middle class through the ownership of land was possible for all. As the land along the coast filled up, people wanted more land in the west in which to grow. Here a man's worth was determined by his ability to work and fight to make his home. This freedom led to the spirit of individualism in the English colonies that was found nowhere else in the world.

In contrast, the French were small in numbers and scattered over a larger area from Canada to Louisiana. Although the French began settlements in 1605, they spent more time exploring and trading with the Indians than in building towns and farms. By 1750 the French numbered only 80,000 in all of North America. The French colony of New France (Canada) had only two towns and both Montreal and Quebec were not very large. In Louisiana, New Orleans was still only a frontier settlement. Between these two French colonies were only a few settlements and a basically friendly Indian population. The King of France ruled his American empire very strictly through an Intendant (Governor) selected by himself. There were few freedoms. Laws were made in France and were to be obeyed by everyone. Only Roman Catholics could come to New France, for there was no freedom of religion. Land could not be owned by an individual for in theory it was owned by the king. Farmers had to rent the land from a landlord who held the land for the king.

As the French and the English struggled over control of the land, each had their own particular advantages. The French had one single authority, the governor; and when he gave orders, they were to be obeyed. The English, on the other hand, had thirteen colonial governors with no coordination. Besides, these governors had to abide by the laws of the local assemblies that controlled the money and the raising of troops. Therefore, The French could organize for war much more quickly.

Secondly, The French relied upon trained soldiers to protect their colonies. Professional soldiers had been stationed in New France since 1661. By 1755, five thousand French soldiers were stationed in New France. Furthermore, the French farmers had been given guns by the King for hunting and defense. If called by the governor, 20,000 French militia could be added to these troops. The English colonies had no trained soldiers although each colonist was expected to serve in the militia. However, no law could force them into military service.

Thirdly, the French had strong allies among the Indian tribes. Since the days of the early explorers the French had been friendly to the Indians. Missionaries like Father Marquette and Father Hennepin had made efforts to Christianize the Indians. Fur trappers and traders had lived with the Indians and even married and had children with Indian women. In spite of many hardships the French had worked hard to gain Indian friendship.

By contrast the English had not found the Indian to be a worthy brother. With the exception of the Iroquois, who the English viewed as too powerful, the English colonists were determined to push out the Indians even when some Indians tried to live like the English. Several wars were fought over land ownership with the Indian's eventual loss. Indians never could understand the English view of land ownership and tended to side with the French, who did not take their land.

The English had some advantages too. There were many more settlers than the French and they lived in more thickly settled areas which could be easily defended. There were also some large towns like New York and Philadelphia that could produce some goods and supplies. Also, the French may not have understood that the English colonists had many freedoms that they were willing to fight for. They believed in the right to own land, practice their own industry or trade and some basic concepts of liberty. If provoked, the colonists would fight for these freedoms.

Economically the English had the advantage as well. The thirteen colonies were self-sufficient; New France was not. The longer and colder winters in Canada meant that the growing season was shorter. Supplies had to be sent to Canada each year. To make matters more difficult, the St. Lawrence River was the only supply route from France and this could be blocked by the British navy. To protect this Breton Island. It was called Louisbourg, after King Louis XIV, and was the strongest fortification in North America. It was built from stone that had been carried over from France. If the furs could not be sent to France and the trade goods brought in for the Indians, the Indians might see little reason to fight for the French.

CHAPTER 2

EIGHTEENTH CENTURY WARFARE

A brief look at the wars fought in the sixty years prior to 1750 reveal two methods of fighting. Since the Middle Ages, Europeans made war according to a system of unwritten rules. Many of these rules had been handed down from the days of chivalry. The Indians did not know these rules, nor would they have wanted to learn them, but Indians did have their own system of rules. These two systems will now be examined.

The Indian code of war was very simple: be brave and bear torture without flinching or crying out. The Indian population of North America was very small. When the Iroquois Confederacy was formed around 1550, their population was about 5500 people. At no time did their population ever exceed 15,000. The Iroquois were the strongest and best organized of any of the woodland Indians but seldom had more than 2000 warriors at any time. Indian lives were too precious to squander away in useless battles and so Indian tactics developed with this idea. The Iroquois lived in the finger lakes area of present day New York state.

The Indians of Canada were mostly Algonquin tribes and were enemies of the Iroquois and generally allied with the French who provided them with guns as a balance against the Iroquois. Indians in the Ohio Valley were generally friendly with the Algonquin as well because they feared the power of the Iroquois.

Indian chiefs held an honorable position, they were not hereditary. When war was declared, the war chief would recruit his own volunteers and conduct his own expedition. Warriors were under no obligation to go to war and if they did, they had to provide their own food, weapons and supplies. Indian weapons consisted of a bow and arrows, tomahawk and war club. A war club was about two feet long with a heavy ball attached to the end. Some Indians even wore armor made of woven reeds around their body and legs. As guns were traded from the Europeans, many exchanged their bows for guns and the armor was discarded. Each warrior carried a supply of charred corn ground into flour and mixed with maple syrup. This was his food ration until food could be captured from the enemy.

Indians did not have ranks of leadership. If several chiefs combined into a large war party, each chief led his own warriors. They marched single file through the forest with scouts ahead to detect ambushes. Attacks were always planned to be quick. A raid upon an enemy village would have the objective of capturing prisoners and taking scalps. Indians also traveled by canoe where rivers and lakes were accessible.

Once an Indian felt that he had proven his bravery or he felt that his side had lost a battle, he would go home. Indians were individualist and had no loyalty to anyone except a chief that might persuade him to his side. Land ownership meant nothing to the native Indians but they were aware of the growing English colonies that continued to push into their hunting grounds.

The Indian method of warfare influenced the America spirit of individualism. Although war bands fought together, each warrior fought separately. An individual warrior would fight his enemy one to one. If possible the dead enemy would be scalped before the attack upon the next opponent. This type of fighting would show an individual courage, which was more important than discipline. A pitched battle was avoided and victory was usually achieved by surprise attacks and ambushes. Once the advantage had been gained, hand to hand combat took place. If the advantage was lost, warriors would slip away and escape. Any man, woman or child that was not slaughtered was taken prisoner.

If an Indian was captured he knew he would not be reclaimed. Indians seldom exchanged prisoners, making the fate of any prisoners to be either adoption by the tribe or death. Being able to show bravery in the face of death was admired in enemies. The three most common methods of killing prisoners was torture, being burnt alive or being cooked and eaten. Torture could last for several days and was usually done by the women of the tribe. A typical torture might be to pull out all of the fingernails, hang red-hot axes around the neck, pour boiling water over the head, cut off pieces of flesh and roast them before the victim's eyes and finally to tear out the heart and eat it. If the victim had been very brave, eating the heart was believed to give the captors courage.

Since Indians valued their life in battle, they usually sought cover. Fighting from behind trees and rocks is called open formation. It is also called Indian style or forest style fighting. Indian attacks upon the white settlers followed this pattern: a surprise raid upon the settlement was made often before sunrise. Captives would be taken and anyone who could not keep up with the Indians would be killed. Then when the settlers organized a pursuit force to recapture the prisoners, the Indians awaited in ambush. The captives then became the wives and children of warriors who had lost their wife of child and the men were tortured.

European armies were recruited for the king. Regiments were formed and were controlled by wealthy nobles who were given allowances for the recruitment, equipment and pay for the soldiers. If any money was left over after these expenses, the noble could keep it. Criminals, beggars and the worst of society were usually recruited into the army since they were the easiest and cheapest to recruit. The usual method of recruitment was by force and fraud. Often criminals were given the choice of prison or serving in the army. To keep these men in order, discipline had to be harsh. Usual punishments included running the gauntlet, riding a wooden horse with a musket ties to each leg, strapping a cannon ball to an ankle, or being whipped with a cat-of-nine tails. In 1712 a British guardsman was ordered 12,600 lashes. He nearly died after receiving 1800 and had to recover before receiving more.

The infantry was drilled in marching and musketry. Each man was expected to stay in step, keep straight lines and follow orders. This was essential for the battle formation. The main weapon was a flintlock musket with a socket bayonet. The musket fired a round lead ball which had to be loaded down the barrel. Some twenty steps were necessary to reload and a soldier was expected to be able to reload and fire about three times per minute. The musket was very inaccurate and seldom could hit an aimed target beyond 100 yards. Because of this, the entire platoon or regiment, would fire at once in the same direction and aiming was not necessary. This is called volley firing. The musket weighed about ten pounds and about sixty pounds of equipment was carried in his back pack. The government supplied rations, tents and clothing. A bakery and other supplies were carried in wagons. A balanced army also had artillery and cavalry. Roads were necessary to get supplies to the troops and fortresses were built to store the supplies and serve as bases. In combat, the troops were expected to move from a column of four on a road into lines of three facing the enemy as quickly and as orderly as possible. It took the British army six hours to do this at the Battle of Blenheim in 1704. Since it took so long to maneuver and prepare for battle, no fight ever took place that both commanders weren't expecting. During the battle, platoons would mass together in lines of three and fire a volley. The more volleys fired the more smoke there was and so the European armies wore brightly colored uniforms so they could know who was friend from foe. The British Army chose red for their uniforms and the French chose White. Under cover of the smoke and to the sound of drums a bayonet charge when then be made. While the hand to hand combat ties down the infantry, the cavalry would try to charge the weakest place in the enemy line; which was often a flank or rear, to win the victory. This is called linier tactics. Its chief advantage is in mass fire power. However, whoever fired first was at a disadvantage since the enemy would then fire at a closer range.

The crucial test of the soldiers was the ability to hold their fire until the enemy was within 50 yards or less. At Blenheim, the French held their fire until the British were 30 yards away. The British then advanced to the French defenses and fired into the faces of the French. Precision and discipline was very important. At the Battle of Fontonoy in 1745, a British captain named Lord Charles Hay marched ahead of his men and courteously challenged the French to fire first after both sides had lined up in the open in front of each other.

Artillery was best used to attack fortifications and usually played minor roles on the battlefield. Since it was hard to find food for the men and horses in the winter, fighting usually stopped in December and began again in the spring. An eighteen-century campaign in Europe was often long and drawn out. As long as military technology did not change, the rules of war did not change.

The English colonists had lived near the Indians for over a hundred years and they were familiar with the Indian tactics. The colonists soon learned to fight like Indians and developed this sense of independence. They did not wear colorful uniforms but often wore green or brown hunting shirts and learned to travel lightly through the woods. They did practice drill and musketry in lines in their own towns but seldom would fight in this manner. They did not fight for pay but did expect to receive some food rations while away from their homes. Like the Indians, they would return home when the war was over.

From 1689 to 1815 Britain and France fought a series of wars known as the Second Hundred Years War. The first three wars started in Europe and later the colonists went to war in America. In America, the wars were named for the reigning monarch and had different names in Europe.

In America	Date	In Europe
King William's War	1689-1697	War of the League of Augsburg
Queen Anne's War	1702-1713	War of the Spanish Succession
King George's War	1744-1748	War of the Austrian Succession
French and Indian War	1754-1763	Seven Years War

The other wars were the American Revolution (1775-1783), the French Revolution (1789-1799) and the Napoleonic Wars (1799-1815). The first three wars began in America with French and Indian raids upon some English settlements followed by the English colonist's attacking some of the French forts.

No important changes resulted from these wars except that Nova Scotia was kept by the British government after Queen Anne's War. No British soldiers were used in America in these wars as the colonists proved capable of defending themselves. If British soldiers had been used it would have been an insult to the colonist's ingenuity. Later British soldiers will look upon the colonials as troops who lacked discipline and were cowards in a fight because they hid behind cover, Indian Style.

North America is mostly made up of forests and different than Europe which is mostly plains. Cavalry is eliminated for lack of fodder and there were few roads to carry supplies. Being able to move quickly and lightly was a major advantage in America. A simple wooden fort can control key areas since artillery is difficult to move against it. The French knew these advantages and learned to fight in open formation. The British, having success in Europe with linier tactics will follow the European way to fight a war.

By 1750 it was becoming evident that a show down was near. The arrival of the British Army will help win the struggle, but will upset the independent minded colonials. American individualism will be at risk. The French and Indian War will change the world and a young Virginia colonist named George Washington will start this great world war.

CHAPTER 3

GEORGE WASHINGTON AND THE FRONTIER

King George's war ended in 1748 and the peace treaty returned any captured territory back to its previous owners. The colonists had captured the French fortress of Louisbourg with their own blood and enterprise, but it had to be given back. The French realized that their settlements in Canada and Louisiana needed to be strengthened and more closely connected. So, in 1749 orders were given to the French soldiers to begin building a string of forts from Lake Erie to the Ohio River.

In 1748 a wealthy Virginian named George Mercer was given a grant of 200,000 acres of land in the Ohio Valley by King George II. More English settlers were coming to America and the king had decided to control the new immigration. Mercer needed someone to build a fort in Ohio, staff it with soldiers and negotiate with the Indians. So, he asked his friend Thomas Lee for help and Lee organized a stock company to raise funds called the Ohio Company. We will make note of two of the new stock holders, Robert Dinwiddie and Lawrence Washington. Dinwiddie was the governor of Virginia and Washington was a large land owner in northern Virginia, both hoped to improve their wealth with this investment. Lee had already negotiated a treaty with the Indians in the Shenandoah Valley and it was believed that he could do the same in the Ohio country.

Lawrence Washington owned a tobacco plantation he called Mount Vernon after Admiral Edward Vernon, of the British Navy, who he had served under as a volunteer when he was young. Lawrence held a position of colonel in the Virginia militia and was a member of the House of Burgesses and had connections with Dinwiddie. Lawrence was also plotting out the new town of Alexandria, Virginia and had given a job to his younger half-brother, George, to survey the town lots. George could also employ his surveying skills for the Ohio Company. In 1752 Lawrence died of tuberculosis. George was already managing Mount Vernon but soon inherited the property.

Governor Robert Dinwiddie was in a position to improve his business interests. As governor he commissioned William Trent, an Ohio Company employee, a captain in the Virginia Militia and instructed him to recruit a company of men and build a fort at the forks of the Ohio River (where the Allegheny and Monongahela Rivers meet). Trent once had a trading post there but had recently abandoned it. Trent set out in the summer of 1753 with 40 men to build the fort. That same year over 1000 French soldiers were ordered by the French Governor Duquesne to proceed to the forks of the Ohio and also build a fort.

The French had problems supplying so many men and they never reached the forks of the Ohio that summer. Instead they had built three forts to serve as bases and prepared to move to the Ohio the next year. Trent heard about the French actions and informed Dinwiddie. Dinwiddie then decided to send a message to the French commander at these forts to protest their occupancy of English lands. Dinwiddie selected 21-year-old George Washington to deliver the message. Washington was commissioned a major in the Virginia militia to improve his status in meeting with the French.

Washington set out on his mission in November, 1753; hardly a good time of the year for such a journey in the wilderness. Crossing rugged mountains, difficult trails, through rain and snow he finally delivered the warning to the French in December. The French reply was a cordial refusal to leave the area. Washington's return to Virginia was worse than his trip to western Pennsylvania. After escaping an Indian assassin and nearly drowning in the Allegheny River, he finally arrived back in Williamsburg, Virginia in January 1754. What he told Dinwiddie assured the governor that the Ohio country was going to have to be held by force.

Washington was now promoted to Colonel and instructed to recruit 150 men to proceed to the forks of the Ohio in the spring. He was to reinforce the men building the fort under Trent's command. His command would be paid with land from the Ohio Company.

Washington set out in in April, 1754. About half way there they met Trent and his men returning to Virginia. Washington was told how 500 French soldiers with about as many Indians had forced the small fort to surrender. The French were now building Fort Duquesne at the forks. Washington pressed on and when he arrived at the Great Meadows he decided to stop and build a fort. Here he would wait for additional reinforcements while Trent went back to Virginia to inform Dinwiddie of the situation.

Washington's fort at the Great Meadows he called Fort Necessity. It was built in a circular shape, not as a strong position but merely as a safe place to store his supplies. The men would sleep in tents outside the fort and dug a few trenches for defense. It was not a particularly good location for a fort but the open space of the meadow prevented the enemy from getting close to his position without being seen.

Soon Washington heard that a small party of French soldiers were raiding a few of the settlements of the Ohio Company, so he set off with fifty men to try to find out what was going on. On May 28,1754 Washington's men with the help of forty Indians surprised a force of thirty-two Frenchmen along Chestnut Ridge. Just after dawn George Washington gave the order to open fire on the French who were just awaking for the morning. After a quick firefight, the French commander Captain Joseph de Coulon de Jumonville was killed and the French surrendered. One French soldier escaped, but ten were killed and the rest were taken prisoner. Washington had lost one man.

The skirmish with the French is today called the Battle of Jumonville Glen. Washington had just started the French and Indian War. The French soldier that had escaped soon reached Fort Duquesne and informed the French officials there what had happened.

A force of 500 French and Indians soon set out to seek revenge. They were led by Jumonville's brother, Louis Coulon de Villiers. Expecting the French, Washington was improving the defense at Fort Necessity. He had just received 250 men as reinforcements and the news that his superior, Colonel Fry, had recently died back in Virginia. He was now the highest-ranking officer in the Virginia militia.

On July 3, 1754, the French and Indians arrived at Great Meadow and began to surround Washington's forces. Washington ordered his men into lines in front of the fort to await the French attack; but there was no attack. The Indians began firing from behind the trees and the Virginians headed for the trenches. It was a one-sided affair and by mid-afternoon it began to rain. Washington's men had taken several casualties and now most of their powder was wet. His men had few bayonets and if the French and Indians closed in after dark they would be no match in hand to hand combat. Realizing the precarious situation, he was in, Washington decided he could not win a battle at this place. Around nightfall Washington began to negotiate with the French. The terms would allow him to march out with the honors of war. They could carry their muskets and wounded and return to Virginia. They could not return to this area for a year and must return the Jumonville Glen prisoners.

The surrender document was written in French and poorly translated so when Washington signed it he did not realize he was admitting to being the assassin of Jumonville. The document eventually arrived in

Paris and was used as propaganda for the official declaration of war. Washington had admitted in writing that he had committed a criminal act. The document was signed after at 8 pm. July 3, 1754 and George Washington had started the the French and Indian War and declared in writing that he was a criminal.

CHAPTER 4

THE ALBANY CONFERENCE

Virginia was not the only colony concerned about the advance of the French into the Ohio Valley. The colonies north of Virginia had often come under attack by the French and Indians in the three previous wars. With the threat of war approaching, a conference was called to be held at Albany, New York. In June 1754, while George Washington was building Fort Necessity, delegates from seven colonies met. The main item of business was whether the Iroquois would be on the side of the English colonies if war broke out with the French.

The colonies had much to fear from the Iroquois. If the Iroquois sided with the French the entire northern frontier could be rolled back to the coast. The Iroquois strength was based on their organization. The Iroquois were actually six nations, the Mohawks, Oneidas, Onondagas, Cayugas and the Senecas. In 1713 the Tuscaroras joined the Iroquois Confederacy. They are shared a common language and culture and would fight together like a unified nation.

For several hundred years the Iroquois had increased their power through war with their neighbors. The surrounding Indians were of the Algonquin language, but they were not united like the Iroquois. Those who were not ruled by the Iroquois either paid tribute or moved farther west to avoid their control. Iroquois control extended from Canada to the Tennessee River and west to the Mississippi River. The Iroquois were feared by all of the woodland Indians.

When the French arrived in Canada they treated the Algonquin tribes with fairness and created a lasting friendship. In 1609 Samuel de Champlain accompanied an Algonquin war party against the Iroquois. Champlain used guns during the battle and helped defeat the Iroquois. It was the first time Indians had seen guns. Since that time the Iroquois became hereditary enemies of the French.

Wars between the Iroquois and Algonquin had existed for centuries. Now the English and French were being brought in to their conflict. King William's War began after an Iroquois attack had been made against the French. To show their power to the western tribes, the Iroquois raided and massacred the village of Lachine near Montreal in 1689. The next year saw French and Indian raids upon the English colonies in retaliation.

The hatred and rivalry was further extended because of the fur trade. The Iroquois found that the fur business was a way to receive English trade goods and guns. The Indians to the west were either trading with the French or with the Iroquois. Attacks upon fur traders were carried out by both sides. A successful raid against the French convoys along the Great Lakes could be devastating to the economy of French Canada.

Although the Iroquois hated the French they did not see the English as their friends. The Iroquois tried to play the French against the English because they did fear the growth of the English colonies. The colonists were numerous and encroaching on their lands. So, the Iroquois went to Albany to complain about the loss of their land. The Iroquois chiefs were present at the Albany Conference and agreed not to support the French in any French-English war. In return, they wanted William Johnson to represent them in their dealings with the British government. Johnson was unlike most English settlers. He was an Irishman who had married an Indian woman. He lived near the Iroquois and treated them fairly. He was honest with the Iroquois and they trusted him.

Once the Iroquois question was settled the chiefs went home. News of Washington's surrender at Fort Necessity had recently arrived and some of the delegates decided to talk more about the frontier situation. Then Benjamin Franklin proposed to the remaining delegates that the colonial governments should get together and form an alliance. His proposal is called the Albany Plan of Union. The purpose of the union would to be cooperate for war if necessary. Some of Franklin's plan was borrowed from the Iroquois confederacy. However, Franklin's plan called for a federal form of government.

Franklin's plan called for a president-general to be appointed by the king to lead the thirteen colonies. A grand council would be appointed by the colonial assemblies based in proportion to the taxes each colony contributed. Together the president-general and the grand council would have the power to make Indian policy for all of the thirteen colonies. They could negotiate treaties, declare war and peace, regulate trade, build forts, raise armies and control the settlement of the west. To accomplish this, they would have the power to levy taxes. The delegates enthusiastically approved the Albany Plan and went home to get it passed in the colonial assemblies.

Every colony rejected the Albany Plan. The colonies did not want to give up their independence by allowing a higher power the ability to tax them. They believed that taxation was their exclusive power. It is doubtful that the British government would have approved it anyway. The threat from the French and Indians was not great enough to threaten their independence. However, twenty years later the threat of unfair taxation and unjust laws will move the colonies to union.

Benjamin Franklin was a man ahead of his time. His Albany Plan of Union was a closer federal union than the thirteen colonies were willing to make even during the Revolutionary War. Not until 1787 will the independent minded American be willing to accept federalism, and then only after many setbacks.

Although the friendship of the Iroquois had been achieved, the thirteen colonies will fight or not fight the war their own way. No British commander will be able to raise troops or money in any colony without the consent of the colonial assembly. Some colonial troops will not be able to serve outside of their own colony. Pennsylvania, under Quaker leadership, will not even vote any money for its own defense. Under this situation the British government will have to provide more money and troops to defend the colonies. Who will have to pay for this additional expense? The failure of the Albany Conference to unify the colonies will plant the seeds of the end of the English colonies in America. But first, a war will have to be fought with British commanders and armies sent to America.

CHAPTER 5

GENERAL BRADDOCK AND THE LESSONS OF WAR

Now that war with France had begun Governor Dinwiddie appealed to the British government for help. In 1755, General Edward Braddock arrived from Ireland with two regiments of British regulars. At sixty years of age Braddock had forty-five years of army experience and his troops were veterans trained in the rules of war. His orders were to march to the forks of the Ohio and capture Fort Duquesne. Braddock began by asking Virginia to supply his army for war.

George Washington volunteered to be Braddock's aide and was sent ahead to organize the wagons and supplies. However, Virginia is a colony with few roads and was unable to provide enough wagons and horses. Food supplies were also lacking because much of Virginia grew tobacco rather than edible crops. So, General Braddock had to ask other colonies for help. Benjamin Franklin came to Braddock's aid by providing the army with the needed supplies. He persuaded many Pennsylvanians to provide horses, wagons and food stuff by appealing to their pocket books. For these supplies the people of Pennsylvania received over $100,000 in gold and silver of the king's money. This money was badly needed in the near barter economy of Pennsylvania.

To show what a British officer required for his personal supplies just take a look at this list:

6 lbs. Loaf sugar	1 Gloucester chees
6 lbs. Muscovado sugar	1 keg (20 lbs.) butter
1 lb. green tea	2 doz. Madeira wine
1 lb. bohea tea	2 gals. Jamaica spirit
6 lbs. ground coffee	1 bottle of mustard
6 lbs. chocolate	2 cured hams
50 lbs. of biscuits	6 dried tongues
8 oz. pepper	6 lbs. rice
1 qt. white wine vinegar	6 lbs. raisons

Of course, officers demanded more than the common soldier, but one can see the huge logistical problem that needed to be overcome.

Braddock's force of 2200 men set out on April 26, 1755 with the plan to take Fort Duquesne and then swing north and capture Fort Niagara. This was a very ambitious plan that had been worked out in England without thinking about the geography of North America. Two other armies made up of colonial troops from New York and New England were also to attack Niagara and Montreal. Braddock had no idea what was ahead of him. When told that the Indians would be helping the French, Braddock replied, "These savages may, indeed, be a formidable enemy to raw American militia, but upon the King's regular and disciplined troops, sir, it is impossible they should make any impression."

George Washington advised that pack horses should carry the supplies but Braddock insisted that a road must be built for the wagons. Three hundred ax men worked ahead of the army felling trees and dragging away the boulders. The army only traveled four miles a day with the men marching a hundred yards and then resting while more road was completed.

The march was too slow and the supplies were being used up too fast, but the Indians did not attack. In fact, they were rarely even seen. Scouts moved ahead of the army and along the sides and had plenty of time to warn of any attacks. Although the Indians were well aware of the approach of Braddock's army, they had never see a force so large and well organized.

About half way to Fort Duquesne it became obvious that Braddock would have to move faster since it was rumored that Fort Duquesne would soon receive reinforcements. George Washington proposed that the army be split into two groups. The first to move rapidly forward using pack horses, with the wagons to follow in the second group. Taking this advice, Braddock left Colonel Dunbar with half the army and the wagons and told him to come up at his own speed. With the remainder (about 1400 men) Braddock hurriedly advanced upon the forks. As Braddock approached his destination he realized that the best place for troops to be attacked would be as they crossed the Monongahela River just a few miles from Fort Duquesne. So, he sent Colonel Thomas Gage ahead with a picked force to take the crossing but no French were defending that position.

On July 9, 1755, the British regulars and Virginia militia crossed the Monongahela only eight miles from Fort Duquesne. The army band played the "Grenadiers March" as the army crossed the river having no fear of an enemy attack. The army marched in a twelve-foot wide corridor with the advance troops marking the trees that would have to be cut down for the road. The column stretched for 1900 yards when disaster struck.

The Indians had been following Braddock all along. The mere size of Braddock's force had been enough to keep the Indians from attacking. At Fort Duquesne Captain Daniel Beaujeu knew that the fort would fall if he did not attack the British, and by tomorrow it would be too late. But the Indians would not go with him. So Beaujeu took 250 Canadians and dressed Indian fashion (buckskins and no shirt) and decided to attack the British while they crossed the river. For several hours, he persuaded the Indians to join him by taunting them with anger and shame. Finally, about 650 Indians decided to join the one man whose courage they admired.

Beaujeu did not reach the river in time, nor did he set an ambush. The French and Indians stumbled upon the British scouts and pushed them into the leading British troops and so began the wilderness Battle of Monongahela. Beaujeu directed the Canadians to hold the center and the Indians to attack the British flanks. The French and Indians took cover amongst the trees and began firing individually. The British formed a double line with the front-rank kneeling and fired a volley into the trees ahead. With European disciple, three volleys were fired at an unseen enemy. Then the Indians stopped firing. Captain Beaujeu had been shot in the head and killed and the Indians were now leaderless. A British bayonet charge may have won a victory but the British were not sure what to do when the firing had stopped. Colonel Gage now ordered up two small cannons and began firing into the forest only to hear war whoop in the woods.

Captain Jean Dumas, the French second in command, gave the war whoops that brought the Indians back to their task. Firing from behind rocks and trees the Indians soon began taking a toll of the packed British ranks. More British troops came forward and collided with those already in lines. As officers were killed, orders were not being given and the soldiers did not know how to fight on their own. The French and Indians could not miss and could not been seen for the forest and the smoke. The European trained fighting machine could not make independent decisions. Only the Virginians broke for cover and they were often fired upon the redcoats who mistook them for Indians.

As Braddock rode up he ordered the Virginians into lines. Several attacks were ordered, but not enough men would follow the officers. The regulars were afraid of the Indians, hearing stories of scalping and torture, and sought the safety of a large crowd. By now firing could be heard far to the rear and panic set in upon the redcoats. Braddock had four horses shot from under him. He was hitting his men with his sword trying to bring back some order, when a bullet fell him from his fifth horse. He was carried off the field by a few officers. By this time the entire British force had been routed, the men in panic.

Of the 1459 officers and men, 456 were dead and 421 were wounded. There was no pursuit as the French and Indians began scalping and looting the dead. Washington was the only officer who was not killed or wounded. He had two horses shot from under him and bullet holes in his hat and coat.

Braddock had ordered the retreat, but the men ran so fast that all of the supplies, guns, money and even the British plans were left behind. Four days later, Braddock died. George Washington conducted the funeral and he was buried in the road he had so painstakingly built. The army then marched over his grave so the Indians could not find it and dig it up. Colonel Dunbar, taking command, retreated all the way back to the coast and then to Philadelphia, leaving Virginia defenseless. European style tactics had been defeated in the wilderness of America.

The individualism of the open formation had beaten the disciplined soldier not trained to do their own thinking. That was the lesson of the Battle of Monongahela. One of the last things General Braddock said was, "We shall better know how to deal with them another time." We will soon examine those who learned this lesson and those who chose to ignore it. Even George Washington in later years will try to build a conventional army. Wagon driver Daniel Morgan will teach this lesson to the British again, twenty-five years later. Daniel Boone, also a wagon driver, will be a smarter man when he returns to the wilderness of Kentucky. Individualism in warfare like individualism of American liberty is an adaption of the American environment.

CHAPTER 6

THE ACADIANS

At the conclusion of Queen Anne's War in 1713 Acadia was given to England and was renamed Nova Scotia. However, the people that lived there were French and generally left alone. They were mostly peasant farm families who had not taken part in Queen Anne's War. They were called the neutral French.

The British government neglected the Acadians. The only requirement they had to fulfill was swear allegiance to the king of England. They were allowed to keep their Catholic religion and their bishop was still appointed in France. During King George's War the Catholic priests were influential in stirring up the Indians to attack the British. Attacks were made against Annapolis Royal in 1744, but few Acadians took part.

In 1755, the governor of Nova Scotia was Charles Lawrence. He complained that for the past forty years the Acadians had not been good British subjects. He feared that they might become active enemies now that war had broken out in the Ohio Valley. There were more than 6000 Acadians but he had only about 650 soldiers divided into three forts to protect Nova Scotia from the French and Indians. He naturally felt threatened, especially if the Acadians joined with the regular French forces from Canada. In June, two thousand New England troops joined the British forces and they captured the French forts along the border with Nova Scotia and Canada. Among the prisoners were 200 Acadians. This was the last straw for Governor Lawrence.

According to Governor Lawrence the Acadians could not be trusted. They had broken the oath to King George II, helped French soldiers and aided French Indians. The parish churches must be houses of treason. With the king's permission, Lawrence gave an order that all Acadians must be rounded up and cast out of Nova Scotia. From September to December some 6000 Acadians were rounded up by the soldiers (colonial and British). Many were placed in the thirteen colonies where their reception was not always pleasant. Some arrived in Louisiana and are today called "Cajuns." Henry Wadsworth Longfellow in his poem "Evangeline" described their plight:

> You are convened this day by his Majesty's orders. Clement and kind has he been; and how have you answered his kindness? Let your hearts reply! To my natural make and temper. Painful is the task I do, which to you I know must be grievous. Yet must I know and obey, and deliver the will of the monarch: Namely, that all your lands, and dwellings, and cattle of all kinds forfeited be to the crown; and that you yourselves from this province be transplanted to other lands. God grant that you may dwell there ever as faithful subjects, a happy and peaceable people. Prisoners now I declare you; for such is his Majesty's pleasure!

At the end of the war about 1500 will return to Canada or Nova Scotia.

The dispersal of the Acadians was an act of war based on military necessity, but a free and independent people should not be treated in such a way. Even the New England troops in Nova Scotia sensed that this was wrong. However, knowing their Puritan background, this guilt was soon forgotten since they were helping to drive out Catholics.

Also, New England families were given the Acadian lands they vacated. Doesn't the law of England apply to the colonies? What about due process and the rights of free men? Surely the thirteen colonies could see to what extent the British government would go to control a rebellious colony. Here is another lesson of history.

CHAPTER 7

UNDECLARED WAR CONTINUES

The lessons of linear tactics versus open formations were yet to be learned in 1755 by others. With General Braddock's death, the command of British forces in America now belonged to William Shirley. Shirley was governor of Massachusetts and had planned the successful capture of Louisbourg in 1745. He always wanted to lead troops, now he had his chance, but he had little experience. With an army of 1500 New Englanders he planned to attack Fort Niagara where General Braddock was to meet him.

A second army of 3000 New Englanders and New Yorkers were under the command of William Johnson. His plan was to attack the French fort at Crown Point on Lake Champlain and thereby control the route to Montreal. Johnson entertained about 1100 Iroquois at his home near Albany to get them to join him. After ten days of speeches, refreshments and exchanging wampum only about 300 Indians went with Johnson's army. It had taken much skill and understanding to get even these to join. It was no surprise that the Indians did not go with him. He knew that they would be fighting their relatives who had joined the French.

Both armies started their march in July from Albany. All of the troops were inexperienced colonials and the colonial assemblies were paying for these forces.

When the colonial assemblies approved the funds for these forces they put limits on the governor's control of the army. The governors were not trusted by the assemblies to handle the finances of war as they held their position by appointment of the king. The men were not used to combat or any sort of discipline. These were typical American armies. They were temporary, tough, but also unpredictable. Besides, both commanders had never commanded troops before. Also, Shirley and Johnson did not know that the French already knew their plan. Copies of their plan had been captured at Monongahela.

Shirley's army marched west, but it took it four weeks to reach Lake Ontario. Fort Oswego was the British post on the lake, but it was in bad shape. Here Shirley's army heard of Braddock's defeat and many of his men deserted. Shirley sent some Indian scouts to Fort Niagara while he repaired Fort Oswego. He was also concerned that French forces at Fort Frontenac, across the lake from Oswego, might capture Oswego while he marched to Niagara. When the scouts returned, Shirley learned that Fort Niagara had been reinforced. These were new troops that had arrived from France as the St. Lawrence River was not blockaded by the British navy very effectively. Leaving 700 men to hold Oswego, Shirley abandoned the plan to attack Niagara and returned to Albany. This decision will cost him his position as overall commander and governor of Massachusetts and he returned to England.

William Johnson met with more success. Marching north from Albany he arrived at Lake George, which he named for King George II. About 200 more Iroquois joined him on the way. At Lake George, he began building Fort William Henry as his base before marching to Crown Point. The French, knowing his plan, sent Baron Dieskau with 3000 men and 600 Indians to ambush his army. Dieskau left 1500 men to build a new fort, Ticonderoga, and with the rest of his army marched around behind Johnson.

On September 8, Johnson made a mistake by sending 1000 men to seek out the French. This force marched into an ambush that could have been worse than Monongahela. The French led Indians fired too soon, perhaps to warn their Iroquois cousins of the trap. This became known as the "bloody morning scout." The American troops fell back to Johnson's camp with the French in pursuit. However, the Indians did not like the idea of fighting brother against brother and sat out to watch the rest of the battle.

Dieskau could not command his Indians and they would not follow orders. The Canadians refused to fight in the open to attack colonial troops hiding behind hastily built barricades, and they joined the Indians in the nearby woods. So Dieskau ordered the French regulars to attack the American barricades according to the European rules of war. With drum rolls and fifes playing, the French soldiers marched out in perfect lines. Three white lines with flags and banners flying move forward in perfect step. The first line fired a volley, then the second marched ahead and fired, and then the third. By that time the first line had reloaded, moved to the front and fired another volley.

The Americans were terrified and hid behind the barricades. Some American troops looked out and aimed at an officer. In time, the American militia began firing at the neat rows of French soldiers. Soon the French lines had large holes in them. Dieskau ordered a bayonet charge but there were not enough officers left to carry out the order. A few Americans, led by Phineas Lyman, charged into the woods and engaged the Indians and Canadians. At that point, the French retreated and Johnson won the battle. The untrained American militia had defeated the European linear tactics because of their individualism.

Dieskau had trouble controlling his Indians and Canadians because he did not understand their individualism. Now he was an English prisoner. William Johnson received all of the credit for his victory.

When the king heard of the victory he gave Johnson $25,000 and knighted him. However, it was the colonial themselves that deserved the praise. Without orders and on his own initiative Phineas Lyman turned the tide of battle. With their own equipment and supplies and the cost being paid by their own assemblies the colonists had defeated regular troops. The American colonial troops took their own risks and fired when they wanted to, not when ordered to. To men present at Lake George that day, like Israel Putnam and John Stark, the experience will not be forgotten.

After the battle, the Iroquois left Johnson's army because they were not allowed to torture the prisoners. To replace this loss Robert Rogers volunteered to scout for the army. This was the beginning of a new group called rangers. Roger's Rangers became famous as Indian fighters and raiders and were willing to fight Indian style, or open formation. Even when other soldiers went home for the winter the rangers continued to fight. For the next two months Johnson's army refused to march north and Johnson was content to stay at Lake George. The French defeat, therefore, became a victory since the attack on Crown Point was never made.

European tactics had failed again. However, 1755 was not a good year for the British forces. Indians joined the French and began raids all along the frontier. Many settlements were destroyed and people fled east away from the frontier. By 1758 there will be no settlers west of the Blue Ridge Mountains.

On May 18, 1756 Britain finally declared war on France. The fighting had been going on for two years in America. Now the war became a world war. Britain and France had colonies in Africa and India, and the war will spread there. Europe will also become a battleground as other nations will join in the war. Britain, Hanover and Prussia will fight France, Austria, Russia, Saxony, Sweden and later Spain. In Europe, Prussia, under the leadership of Frederick the Great, will show how a well-disciplined army can win with linier tactics. In America, the British will learn to fight open style. New methods will be used and there will be an increase in the use of rangers. However, to win the war in North America new leadership would be needed; this lesson the British learned at the end of 1755.

CHAPTER 8

FRENCH VICTORIES

Even before war had been declared, the governments of France and Britain were selecting new commanders to send to America. The French chose Louis Joseph, Marquis de Montcalm. His orders were to maintain control of America at all costs. He replied, "I shall do everything to maintain it, or die." The British selected John Campbell, the Earl of Loudoun.

Montcalm was a capable officer who arrived on May 11, 1756 to find the government of Canada full of bribery and corruption. The governor of New France was the Marquis de Vaudreuil. Vaudreuil was Canadian born and had hoped to be selected as general. He was jealous of officers from France and refused to cooperate with Montcalm. Vaudreuil refused to give up his authority over the militia and created a division of the French forces with Montcalm. Montcalm had no authority over the government, only with the regular troops in the military.

Vaudreuil had given much of the government duties over to his head of administration, Francois Bigot, because he wanted to command troops. Bigot created a monopoly in which he could make a profit from the war. Prices for all goods were set by Bigot and he caused corruption of the government through bribery and forgery. He controlled the fur trade and public works. He was responsible for supplying the armed forces and the transporting of arms and equipment. Bigot and his friends were living in luxury while many people were half starved. Vaudreuil knew about Bigot but did nothing about it. Montcalm wrote to a friend in France about Canada in which he said, "What a country, where knaves grow rich and honest men are ruined."

In spite of these difficulties Montcalm proved a capable leader. Eventually the corruption of the government will bring a decline in morale of the Canadian militia who sees his family starving. With Montcalm unable to command the militia and Vaudreuil being uncooperative this became a recipe for disaster.

Lord Loudoun arrived in America on July 23, 1756. He found the disunity of the thirteen colonies preventing him from organizing his command. Colonial assemblies would not provide enough men, money or supplies. Loudoun saw the need for more regular British troops and more financial help. He increased the number of ranger companies and put them directly under his control. A regiment of British regulars was recruited in America and organized by Colonel Henry Bouquet, a Swiss officer serving in the British Army. Other British officers like Lord George Howe and Thomas Gage were experimenting with light infantry, capable of moving more quickly in the forest. Eventually every British regiment would have at least one company that would be light troops. They would cut their coats short and carry less gear to be able to move easier.

In August Montcalm advanced upon Fort Oswego, the British post on Lake Ontario. Outnumbered the British and colonials withdrew inside of the fort which Montcalm put under siege. Montcalm then began digging trenches closer to the fort for an eventual assault while his cannon (captured at Monongahela) fired upon the defenses. Before the assault could be made the British surrendered. The prisoners were sent to Canada but not without a few being massacred by Montcalm's Indians. In one swift attack the British lost control of Lake Ontario and the fleet built by Governor Shirley was captured.

When Lord Loudoun heard about the loss of Oswego he forbids any offensives. The British would remain in place on the defensive. The French appeared to be able to attack anywhere at will. Nearly all of the Indian tribes now joined the French. The Iroquois withdrew from the war and became neutral. Surely the French were going to win. Montcalm had proven his ability to move quickly and achieve decisive results. But Montcalm was unable to do anything else that year for lack of supplies. The corruption of Bigot was affecting the fighting powers of the army.

As 1757 approached, Loudon made plans to attack Louisbourg and Montcalm planned to attack Fort William Henry on Lake George. Loudoun eventually planned to attack Quebec and Montcalm had his sights on Albany. No one made a move until mid-summer.

With 8000 men and 2000 Indians, Montcalm descended upon Fort William Henry in August, 1757. Montcalm began another siege which after just five days resulted in a British and colonial surrender. The siege had been a bluff. The French were short of food and could not stay for a long siege. Montcalm's terms were generous to the surrendered garrison. With a promise not to fight for eighteen months they could go home. However, Montcalm's Indians, many of whom had come from as far away as Iowa, wanted plunder. As the 1400 British and colonial troops marched home, they were attacked by the Indians. Montcalm was unable to control his Indians but was eventually able to stop the massacre. Over 200 prisoners had been killed and another 200 were carried off by the Indians. The Indians took their prisoners to Montreal where the French government had to buy them, but only after one was killed and eaten in the streets of Montreal, much to the disgust of the Canadians.

With the loss of his Indians and the shortage of food, Montcalm called off his attack on Albany and returned to Quebec. Meanwhile, Lord Loudoun prepared to attack Louisbourg, but his army remain stranded in Nova Scotia because of fog and adverse winds. After French ships reinforced Louisbourg, Loudoun cancelled his attack. Then on September 24, 1757 a hurricane wrecked the British fleet.

As 1757 came to a close it looked as if the French would win the war. They had been successful under the leadership of Montcalm in America. The British forces under the Duke of Cumberland had been defeated in Germany. The battlefields of 1757 belonged to the French but other factors were working against France. Canada had two successive crop failures and sixteen supply ships sent from France had been captured. Although 3500 new French soldiers had arrived in Canada they became an extra burden to feed. The people in Quebec were being rationed four ounces of bread and a little salt pork per day. This ration would eventually be cut in half in 1758. A lack of food supplies had handicapped Montcalm for the past two years and if the supply route of the St. Lawrence River did not remain open, the French may have to capitulate. For the British government, it appeared that a new plan was needed. The mistakes of the past year must not be committed again. On June 29, 1757 William Pitt became Prime Minister of Great Britain. Pitt was an honest politician (at a time when most were not) who supported the common people. He became known as the "Great Commoner" for his support of the people who really had very little representation. Under his leadership the British government devised a new plan to win the war.

CHAPTER 9

THE GRAND PLAN

William Pitt recognized that to achieve victory the government must not be afraid to spend money. Since the American colonies could not fund the war themselves, the British government must spend what is necessary for the colonies. Pitt had the idea that the best way to reduce French power would be to attack her colonies and not the strong French army in Europe. The British navy was re-equipped and better organized and the British forces in Germany were withdrawn and sent to America. Since that left Prussia to fight the armies of France, Austria and Russia alone, Pitt agreed to help finance the army of Frederick the Great. Taxes in England were greatly increased and loans were made by the government to finance this plan.

The next part of the plan was to replace the old generals with younger commanders. Lord Loudoun was recalled and replaced by forty-one-year-old Colonel Jeffrey Amherst, who had never held an independent command. Amherst was promoted to major general. To assist him, thirty-one-year-old James Wolfe was made a brigadier general. Their plan of attack was directed against Louisbourg and then Quebec. At the same time, another army would attack Fort Ticonderoga and then advance on Montreal. A third army was to attack Fort Duquesne and Fort Niagara. Pitt requested that the American colonies raise 20,000 troops and sent another 20,000 British regulars to America.

Major General James Abercrombie was given the task of capturing Fort Ticonderoga. Abercrombie was an old European style general who often lacked courage. He had been unable to adjust to the American style of warfare and he was a political appointment of the king's brother. So, Pitt saw to it that Lord George Howe became his second in command. Howe had fought with Roger's Rangers and saw the worth of colonial troops. He had learned to fight forest warfare. Howe gave the army its shape. He eliminated the supply train by having the men carry their own thirty days food rations. He also had the men cut their hair short and shorten their coats to the waist. He equipped men reasonably for the rough work ahead of them. He also did what he could to break down the antagonism between the colonials and the regulars. Pitt hoped that Abercrombie would follow Howe's advice.

With 15,000 men Abercrombie sailed down Lake George in more than 1000 boats. Artillery was placed upon rafts and the entire army sailed in a group over six miles long. As an experiment ten men in every regiment were given rifles. Rifles had been around since the 15th century. They are more accurate than muskets, but they cost more to make and it takes longer to reload. This was the first army ever to be issued rifles. The army landed a short distance from Fort Ticonderoga and proceeded to approach the fort.

Fort Ticonderoga had cost Louis XV a fortune to build. Much of the money going in to the pockets of Bigot and his friends. Although the fort controlled the passage into Lake Chaplain it was not situated on very defensible ground. There was also a shortage of food supplies for the garrison so a siege was not a good idea. Montcalm had only 3200 men and wisely decided not to stay in the fort. About a mile away from the fort, at the top of a hill, he built a log wall with sand bags and decided to defend there.

While Lord Howe was leading the rangers to scout the French defenses he ran into a French force in the woods who were scouting the British. A skirmish was fought and several prisoners were captured, but

Lord Howe was killed. The death of Howe took the spirit out of the men as so many had admired him. With the death of one man, 15,000 would be leaderless. Abercrombie would lead with blind valor now that the soul of the army was gone.

Learning from the prisoners that Montcalm would soon receive 9000 reinforcements, Abercrombie decided that he must attack at once. This information was not true. He made the mistake of leaving his forty cannon on the shore of Lake George and marched directly to Montcalm's defenses. His second mistake was that he attacked Montcalm's prepared defenses head on when he could have gone around them.

Coming out of the woods, the kilted troops of the Black Watch Regiment marched in neat straight lines toward the French defenses. The sound of their bagpipes had the effect of scaring away many of Montcalm's Indians who thought they were hearing the screams of devils; but the French troops were unmoved. They mowed down the neat rows with volley fire. Four more attacks, just like the first were repulsed with severe losses. Abercrombie refused to allow any of his 9000 American troops participate in the battle in any way. With nearly 2000 redcoats littering the battlefield he ordered the army to retreat. Soon the retreat turned into a rout and all of the cannon and supplies were left behind.

Montcalm could not believe the ease of his victory. He had prepared to blow up Ticonderoga and retreat to Montreal. Now he was the victorious general of another battle. The rifle experiment had failed as the rifles were not properly used. Not until the War of 1812 will units be issued rifles again.

Abercrombie still had a large army but refused to do anything for the rest of the year. However, he did allow Colonel John Bradstreet to make a daring raid deep into French territory. With 2600 men, Bradstreet crossed Lake Ontario and made a surprise attack upon Fort Frontenac. It was a daring plan that paid off better than anyone expected. Fort Frontenac, defended by only 110 men, turned out to be a storehouse of French supplies intended for the Indians of the Ohio. The French supply line to the Ohio was now disrupted. The French kept their ships for Lake Ontario there as well and they were all destroyed. In one swift move, Bradstreet weakened the French hold of the Ohio Indians and cut New France in two.

Meanwhile, Amherst made his attack upon Louisbourg. The capture of Louisbourg was important because it guarded the entrance to the St. Lawrence River, the French supply line. Louisbourg was also used as a base for French ships to attack New England fishermen. Louisbourg was the strongest and best fortified fortress in North America. The walls of the fort were made of stone, imported from France. They were high and very solid and were surrounded by a wide and deep moat. Over 230 cannon defended the place. Louisbourg had been captured once before by New Englanders during King George's War, but now the place was reinforced and twelve French ships guarded the harbor. The French had 7000 men and intended to oppose any landings upon the jagged shore.

Amherst was a cautious commander. He made careful preparations and did not believe in taking risks. His brigadier, James Wolfe, had a reputation for boldness and was fanatical about military duty. Wolfe was a frail individual. He was sickly looking and a complete opposite of Amherst. They did modify their redcoats to American warfare. The uniforms were shortened with the eliminating of much of the trim as Howe had done. He organized light battalions and added them to the lines which were reduced from three to two rows. Wolfe improved the formation of the light infantry. It is the purpose of light infantry to fight in an extended line, that is, to move in small groups to take cover and fire upon the enemy lines before the attack.

There were only four possible beaches for a landing near Louisbourg. Each beach was defended by the French, so Wolfe planned a feint against three of them while he made the main landing farthest from Louisbourg. On June 8, 1758 Wolfe tried to land in the face of 1200 defending Frenchmen. With heavy casualties Wolfe was about to call off the attack when a few boats landed beyond the French and final pushed them out. The English camp was then made three miles from the town. A formal siege took place and trenches were dug toward the fortress. Siege artillery battered the walls. It was strictly a European style affair with no Indians, ambushes or forest fighting. The French were almost out of food and supplies, so they surrendered on July 26, 1758. This was the turning point of the war.

The final part of Pitt's plan was the attack upon Fort Duquesne. General John Forbes was given command of 5000 colonial troops and 1400 British regulars. The mistakes of Braddock were not to be repeated. Forbes would move in cautious stages building forts to serve as bases along the way. George Washington, commanding a Virginia regiment in Forbes army, approached the general to give him advise. Washington advised Forbes to use Braddock's road as it was still in good shape. He also advised moving with light troops and pack horses to move more quickly. Forbes would have none of it and dismissed Washington out of hand. He would move through Pennsylvania and take his time. Politically this will give Pennsylvania claims to Ohio. Washington was never asked for advise again and would leave the army after the conclusion of this campaign.

Forbes marched all summer, entrenching his camp every night and built forts about every fifty miles. He became ill on the campaign and could not walk or ride so he was carried in a litter swung between two horses. He trained his men to fight like Indians but to stay together. He was counting on the Indians getting tired of waiting. He considered time was on his side.

When it was getting late in the year and Forbes was still a long way from Fort Duquesne he sent a force of 800 men ahead to try to capture the fort by surprise. Outside the fort, however, the English were ambushed with the loss of 273 men. It was another victory like Monongahela. The French, now feeling the shortage of supplies from the loss of Fort Frontenac and feeling that Forbes would have to retreat for the winter, sent most of their men home until spring. Most of the Indians had already gone home, but Forbes had not given up. On November 25, 1758 Forbes arrived at the forks to find Fort Duquesne a pile of ashes. The French blew it up the day before because they knew they could not defend it with only 300 men. A new fort was built by Forbes that he named Fort Pitt, for William Pitt. Forbes died shortly after that. This victory took many of the Indians away from the French. It ended the border attacks and most Indians were now tired of the war; but it also opened up the west for English settlers.

Pitt's plan was working. Fort Niagara still had to be taken and Ticonderoga had to fall before an attack on Montreal could be made. Quebec now lay open to attack from the St. Lawrence. These were the goals for 1759. The British army had made some changes but colonial troops were being used less. Colonial soldiers were looked down upon and their individualism was disgusting to British officers. Also, the colonial assemblies had not provided enough money for the war effort; therefore, the British government was determined to win the war even without the colonies help.

However, the French were not defeated yet. Montcalm still had the loyalty of his regulars although corruption of the Canadian government was ruining the militia. Canadians were starving and the Indians were not such good allies in a long war. The Indians no longer raided the English settlements and their help was questionable. Indians played no part in the major battles of 1758. One year earlier nearly all of the Indians of North America had been fighting with the French but now things had changed.

CHAPTER 10

THE BATTLE OF QUEBEC

William Pitt was determined to defeat the French in Canada. He ordered General Amherst to capture Ticonderoga and then march upon Montreal. His army of 11,000 men were about half colonist. James Wolfe was promoted to major general and given orders to capture Quebec. This would cut Canada off from France for good. Wolfe had only 9000 men and only one company of rangers were colonials. Wolfe did not like colonial troops.

On June 27, 1759, some 168 ships arrived off of Quebec carrying the British forces. This was the largest war fleet to cross the Atlantic until 1917. The French did not think that the British could safely travel the 800 miles of the St. Lawrence from the ocean; but they had, and without the loss of a single ship.

Wolfe camped his army on the Island of Orleans across from Quebec and surveyed the defenses. The city of Quebec, on the north side of the St. Lawrence, was a natural fortification. It was built on a bluff 300 feet above the river. Here the river narrows to less than a mile and was controlled by Quebec's 106 cannon. There were 2000 men in the Quebec garrison. To pass a ship past the city to the west would be difficult and the north shore is sheer cliff for miles. This area was lightly defended and was the only line of communication to Montreal. To the east of the city is the Beauport Shore. At low tide the Beauport Shore is a flat muddy area where troops could be landed. Here were the main French defenses. Earthworks and trenches had been prepared and they were defended by 14,000 troops. At the end of the Beauport Shore is the Montmorenci River which is so swift that it is impossible to cross except at a few well-guarded places. From this information Wolfe had to make his plans.

Montcalm planned to avoid battle. He outnumbered Wolfe's army and intended to take no risks. He was convinced that Wolfe could not get past Quebec by moving upstream and that the Beauport Shore could not be taken. All he had to do was wait until winter when the St. Lawrence freezes over and forces the British to leave. However, the French had a problem amongst themselves. Montcalm and Vaudreuil were at odds with each other. Although some militia had been recruited into Montcalm's regulars to replace earlier losses, Vaudreuil still commanded the militia as a separate command. Also, the 2000 man Quebec garrison was a separate command. Thus, the French army was divided by three commanders who did not work together.

On the night of June 28 Montcalm sent seven ships down the St. Lawrence loaded to the hilt with explosives. The skeleton crews were to light them on fire as they neared the anchored British fleet. If successful the entire British fleet could go up in flames. However, the fire-ships were set on fire too soon by their nervous crews and caused no damage; but the fireworks were spectacular.

Wolfe knew he had little time and had to act quickly. On June 29, he captured Point Levis on the south bank of the St. Lawrence, opposite Quebec. Guns were brought ashore and the city of Quebec was bombarded. The bombardment would last 79 days and destroy much of the town. Now supplies could not be stored in the city for fear of destruction. Although Wolfe could ruin Quebec, he could not win if he could not defeat the French army.

Wolfe spent the month of July trying to bring Montcalm out to fight. He had foolishly divided his army into five groups that could not even support each other, but Montcalm would not move. On July 31 Wolfe decided upon a desperate attack. Two regiments made a landing on the Beauport Shore near the Falls of Montmorenci. He hoped to lure Montcalm out to the mud flats for a battle. However, the frontal attack was repulsed with serious losses.

During August, Wolfe tried to destroy the morale of the Canadian militia. He ordered the Canadian countryside to be laid waste. Crops and farms were destroyed for miles. This was the revenge for years of Indian raids. Some of the militia deserted, many were tired of the inaction, but most no longer had anywhere to go. Wolfe had also become very ill and his time was running out. None of the plans had worked. However, the British fleet had discovered that they could sail past Quebec without much difficulty.

Montcalm sent reinforcements under Louis Antoine Bougainville to watch the British ships that sailed past Quebec. Wolfe decided upon one last chance before the river froze over. He would move his entire army past Quebec and cut the supply line between Quebec and Montreal. For a week, the ships sailed back and forth and Wolfe, with his unusual eyesight, discovered a path up the cliff just two miles from Quebec. He selected this as his place of assault, but it would have to be at night since Bougainville was marching his men back and forth with the ships. On the night of September 12, Bougainville allowed his men a night's rest and did not follow the ships.

It was the night of September 12 that Wolfe had chosen to make the attack. That night the French were also expecting a supply convoy to sneak along the north shore of the St. Lawrence from Montreal. This had been done successfully a few times in the past. With luck for the British the supply boats had been cancelled for that night but the guards had not been told. Instead of French boats, British boats passed the shore that night and they were not disturbed. Arriving at the point, today called Wolfe's Cove, the British landed below the assigned path. Twenty-four men, led by Colonel William Howe, hanging onto vines and branches climbed the 300-foot cliff and overpowered a sleepy guard of 100 Frenchmen. By morning Wolfe's army was blocking the supply lines between Quebec and Montreal. They had even pulled two small cannon up the cliff.

West of the city of Quebec is a flat area called the Plains of Abraham, named for Abraham Martin who farmed it, Wolfe lined up his men in European battle lines. Montcalm had been tricked. He had expected the attack along the Beauport Shore where the British fleet had kept him up all night with a noisy feint. Montcalm marched as many men as he could gather to the Plains of Abraham. Vaudreuil would not send his militia because he felt the real attack would be at the Beauport Shore and the Quebec garrison refused to come out or provide artillery. Montcalm had sent a message to Bougainville to attack the British from behind but he knew he would not arrive in time. A few Canadians and Indians were already firing upon the lines of redcoats from the trees to the north. Wolfe ordered his men to lie on the ground to make smaller targets.

At 10 o'clock Montcalm could wait no longer. He was afraid the British might be digging in across his supply line, and because of the bombardment of Quebec, the city only had one day's supply of food. To the beat of the drums and with banners flying the French advanced. Wolfe ordered his men to stand, but to hold their fire as long as possible. The French fired a volley at 130 yards and then things went wrong. Many Canadians, now in Montcalm's army, dropped to the ground to reload as they had always done. This broke the ranks of the French which was absolutely essential in linier formations. When the French had advanced to within forty paces the British fired their first volley. They advanced ten paces and fired another volley, the most destructive volley ever fired. The first two rows of the French lines disappeared. A bayonet charge made the French flee the field. General Wolfe had been wounded and died within the hour. Montcalm, also wounded, was taken inside Quebec where he died the next day. When Montcalm died the hope of Canada died. With the help of the Canadians and Indians firing from the woods to the north of the battlefield, the French army escaped to Montreal. The city of Quebec surrendered on September 18, 1759.

In only fifteen minutes on September 13, 1759 the fate of the North American continent was decided. A conquest greater than Alexander the Great, Julius Caesar or Napoleon had been achieved by British arms. Each army had about 4500men in the battle, but the superior discipline of the British had won the day. The decisive battle had been fought in an open field with linier tactics. It was actually the only battle fought in America where both sides fought in the open. It will be the most remembered battle in England and the lessons of the forest will be forgotten. History is too important to forget. Quebec was not a typical American battle and the British will have to learn their history lesson over again at Lexington, Concord and Bunker Hill.

Only Montreal remained in French hands. Fort Niagara had fallen to William Johnson on July 25. Nearly 1000 Iroquois were now fighting for the British and had ambushed the French relief force. The result was the "bloody morning scout" in reverse. Amherst captured Ticonderoga on July 26 but Montreal did not surrender until September 9, 1760. New France was no more.

The fate of America had been decided at Quebec. The removal of the French produced two results. The colonies had matured and come of age because of the French and Indian War. Now the spirit of individualism was free to expand into the continent. The other result was about the fate of the Indians. The French had been their friends and now there was no more help. But the Indians had one more chance. That chance came from the Ottawa chief, Pontiac.

CHAPTER 11

PONTIAC AND THE TREATY OF PARIS

When Governor Vaudreuil surrendered at Montreal he was forced to surrender all of Canada and the Ohio country. Although the French and Indian War was over there was still three more years of war in Europe. General Amherst was determined that the remaining French forts should be taken before any peace treaty was made. Robert Rogers was sent with 200 rangers to accept the surrender of Fort Detroit and the other French forts around the Great Lakes. By November 29, 1760 all of Canada was in British hands.

The Indians of the west hoped that the British would treat them better than the French. Indian society had come to depend upon European trade goods and the men hunted with guns instead of bows. British goods in the past had been cheaper than French goods and they hoped business would be good. Most of the Indians had quit the war long before the surrender of Montreal. The Treaty of Easton in 1758 had made friends with the Indians around Fort Pitt. In this treaty, the British had promised not to allow any more settlements west of the Alleghenies. However, the small garrison at Fort Pitt could not stop the settlers that poured west now that the war was over.

The Indian hopes of better treatment by the British was soon smashed. General Amherst ordered no more presents were to be given to the Indians.

He felt that their friendship should not have to be bought. He also ordered that less gunpowder be traded to the Indians. He did not realize the Indians depended on it for hunting. In time, the Indians found that they were not welcome inside the British forts like they had been when the forts were French. Finally, the loss of their land to the white settlers made the Indians angry at the British. These were the reasons for what became known as Pontiac's War.

Pontiac was a war chief of the Ottawa who lived in the Detroit area. Pontiac had told his followers that England wanted to make them slaves, and since the Indians are the most liberty minded people in the world they quickly joined in Pontiac's plans. Pontiac believed that the Indians could only live peacefully with the French who had lived with them and treated them fairly. The French still held Louisiana and the Illinois country and Pontiac believed the French would send an army to help them if the Indians would drive out the British. Thus, he organized the western Indians to drive out the redcoats.

On May 7, 1763 Pontiac tried to capture Fort Detroit but his plan was betrayed and so he was determined to starve the garrison out. Other Indians attacked the British forts in their areas and by June only Fort Pitt and Fort Detroit had not been captured. The frontier was aflame again and about 2000 settlers were massacred that summer. But Indians were never good at sieges and they tried to stop the relief forces rather than attack the forts.

Amherst ordered Colonel Henry Bouquet to bring supplies and reinforcements to Fort Pitt. He also ordered Bouquet to give the Indians blankets infested with smallpox. This was the first attempt by the British at germ warfare. Bouquet's troops, the Royal Americans and the Black Watch, were trained in light infantry tactics. Bouquet had studied Indian warfare as a subordinate to General Forbes and devised a flexible system of extended order. He knew European style tactics had to be improved by learning the lessons of forest warfare.

In July, Bouquet left Fort Ligonier with pack mules carrying supplies and three regiments of British regulars to bring relief to Fort Pitt. On August 5, 1763 Bouquet's force was ambushed about twenty miles from Fort Pitt. A quick bayonet charge forward scattered the Indians and Bouquet set up a defense on a small hill. He ordered the flour sacks on the mules to be unloaded and placed in a circle to build some shelter. Wounded soldiers and the mules were placed inside this makeshift flour sack fort. Soon his command was surrounded but the Indians did not rush into the open to attack this fort. Fighting was sporadic all day and into the night.

As fighting continued the next day, British casualties were mounting and to remain here all day could lead to disaster. Bouquet devised a plan to defeat the Indians and put it in motion around noon. By faking a retreat on one side of the defense he enticed the Indians to charge out of the woods because they felt that the British had broken in panic. However, Bouquet had sent men out on a flank unseen by the charging Indians. A trap had been set. The flankers fired a volley and immediately launched a bayonet charge. At the same time the retreating soldiers turned around and charged as well. The Indians were pursued for two miles and were never given a chance to rally. The Indians on the other side of the hill knew what had happened and fled. The Indians were beaten with tactics for light infantry and the superiority of the Indians to fight in the forest in open order was ended. The French and Indian War had taught the British how to fight Indian style. This battle became known as the Battle of Bushy Run and was to break the Indians for good.

Fort Detroit was relieved by Robert Rogers who brought reinforcements and supplies. The news of Bushy Run had travelled fast and Rogers met no resistance. News was also in the air that the French had made peace with Britain and the French would not be returning.

Pontiac's War was over quickly although Pontiac himself continued to resist until 1766. After Bushy Run most of the Indians made peace separately. Without a confederation of woodland Indians there was no hope of stopping white settlers. In the next five years 30,000 would cross the mountains and take land.

On February 10, 1763, the Treaty of Paris ended the Seven Years War (French and Indian War in America). In Europe, there were no boundary changes but Prussia had established herself as the leader amongst the German states. Great Britain became the undisputed master of the seas and France lost almost all of its colonies.

British territory in North America stretched from the Gulf of Mexico to Hudson's Bay and from the Atlantic to the Mississippi River. France gave to Spain the Louisiana territory west of the Mississippi, including New Orleans, because Spain had lost Cuba to Britain during the war. Britain returned Cuba to Spain in exchange for Florida.

France was allowed to keep two small islands off the coast of Newfoundland so her fishing boats could have a place to dry their catch. France also kept a few islands in the West Indies that were valuable for their sugar crops.

CHAPTER 12

EPILOGUE AND BIOGRAPHIES

The French and Indian War changed the world. Great Britain gained a world empire and now had a world commercial monopoly. But the British government had borrowed upon the prosperity of the future to win the war. A debt of $700 million was added to the debts started from King Williams War. Much of the debt had been for the defense of America. Now the American colonists were expected to pay this debt. But with the French gone the Americans could see no reason to pay for defense. This was the first change in British policy.

The second change began on October 7, 1763 with the "Proclamation of 1763." The King proclaimed that no settlements could be made west of the Appalachian Mountains. Because of Pontiac's War the settlers and Indians would not live together. A large Indian reservation was created. Many colonists (Americans) were furious. The war started because George Washington engaged French troops over the Ohio Company starting new settlements. Now that was all lost.

Over the next twelve years a number of laws would be passed in Parliament to tax the colonists for their own defense. The individualist colonists felt this to be a major intrusion on their freedom and that the king had become a tyrant. The colonists will openly revolt in 1775 and overthrow the British government and become an independent nation.

There was a new hatred of the Indians because of their actions in the war. The massacring of settlers and land disputes settled by the knife was unacceptable. Their military strength was no longer superior in forest fighting. Not even the Iroquois were feared. It would not take long for all of the Indians in North America to be removed to marginal lands and their culture broken.

France was the biggest loser of the war. After losing all of her colonies she no longer had much of a prosperous economy. With huge debts from the war France became bankrupt. With no solution acceptable to the king, the French people rose up and overthrew the king in 1789.

Now let's turn to the lesson of history that was learned or not learned. In 1763 the British government, to save money, reduced the size of the British Army. All of the light infantry units were discharged. These units had learned the lesson of open formations as proven at the Battle of Bushy Run. Although they will be reconstituted in 1770 they did not use the open tactics as demonstrated by their defeat during the retreat to Boston from Concord in 1775. They were used in lines at Bunker Hill, another disaster that could have been avoided if they had learned from history.

The following biographies will show the lesson of history either learned or not:

Daniel Boone, 1734-1820 (chapter 5), was a wagon driver in Braddock's army. He was nearly killed when the Indians attack the wagon column. He was very critical of General Braddock and spoke negatively about him often. His Indian experiences will help him start successful settlements in Kentucky.

Henry Bouquet, 1717-1765 (chapter 8), was a Swiss mercenary who had severed in several different European armies before being commissioned in the British Army in 1754. He recruited the 60th Regiment of foot known as the Royal Americans. The regiment was made up of colonists raised in Pennsylvania. Bouquet served in Forbes command where he learned about open tactics. In 1763, he commanded the relief column approaching Fort Pitt when ambushed. His subsequent victory at the Battle of Bushy Run proved that troops trained in open tactics could defeat the Indians in combat. What if he had commanded the British troops at Lexington and Concord?

Edward Braddock, 1695-1755 (Ch. 5), commanded the British forces marching upon Fort Duquesne in 1755. He arrogantly ignored all warnings about fighting Indians in the wilderness and ordered his men to fight with linier tactics. His defeat was a lesson to all that fighting in stand-up lines is not a good fighting tactic. The following British generals mentioned in this book or fought in the American Revolution also did not learn this lesson: Jeffrey Amherst, James Wolfe, James Abercrombie and William Howe

Robert Dinwiddie 1692-1770 (Ch. 3), was the governor of Virginia in 1753 when he allowed his position in the government to influence his business interests in the Ohio Company. Using a government employee, George Washington, to ask the French to leave land the Ohio Company claimed was done strictly for his own personal interest. That a war was the result of greedy interests should be a good lesson of not mixing government and business interests.

Benjamin Franklin, 1706-1790 (Ch. 4) is well known as a scientist, inventor, statesman and diplomat. In 1754, he was a leading spokesman at the Albany Conference. Recognizing the strength of the Iroquois through their confederation he called for the thirteen colonies to unite together for the good of all. Unfortunately, the individual colonial assemblies did not see his wisdom of a new idea called federalism. The lesson is to not make decisions based on personal bias than on the good for all. As a founding father, Franklin was able to see his federalism come to fruition when the United States wrote the Constitution of the United States in 1787.

Thomas Gage, 1718-1787 (Ch. 5) commanded the lead battalion in General Braddock's army. When French and Indians engaged him at the Battle of Monongahela, he ordered his men into lines. The British lost the battle and were routed back to Virginia. He was not a distinguished military leader but he did work with light infantry tactics in 1758. He was promoted to Commander in Chief of British forces in North America in 1763 and ordered the British attack on Bunker Hill in 1775. He did not learn his lesson from Braddock or from light infantry training as Bunker Hill was a British disaster. He returned to England after Bunker Hill.

William Johnson, 1715-1774 (Ch. 4, 7), is included here not so much for his learning the lessons of history but to show how some people benefit from the actions of others. Because he had earned the trust of the Iroquois and had learned their language and customs he was made the Indian Agent for the British government. This led him to be appointed commander of a British army in 1756, a duty that he was not qualified for. At Fort William Henry, he ordered the "bloody morning scout" that cost the lives of hundreds of men. Then when the French attacked he gave no orders but the colonial troops on their own initiative won the battle that he would receive credit for as well as some financial rewards. Then in 1758 the history books tell us he captured Fort Niagara. Actually, he did, but it was the Iroquois victory against the French troops that we called in this book the "bloody morning scout in reverse" that allowed him to win. From all of this he became one of the largest land owners in New York and a very wealthy man.

Charles Lawrence, 1709-1760 (Ch. 6), was the military governor of Nova Scotia during the French and Indian War. He was appointed to this position because of his family ties to the Duke of Marlboro who got him his appointment from the king. Lawrence distrusted the Acadians and ordered their expulsion without any distinction of loyalty. Thousands of lives were uprooted and changed because of the over bearing power he held. What would have happened to the rebels (patriots) in the American Revolution had they lost? History repeated itself in 1942 when President Roosevelt used the same reasoning as Lawrence to remove the Japanese-Americans to internment camps without due process. Surely, this lesson of history should not be forgotten.

Thomas Lee, 1690-1750 (Ch. 3), is included in our list since he is a patriarch of a distinguished family in American history. His father was one of the earliest settlers to America and his decedents include some famous Americans like Light Horse Harry Lee and Robert E. Lee. His business ambition started the entire chain of events that we call the French and Indian War. He founded and was president of the Ohio Company. Upon his death Lawrence Washington ran the company and then Robert Dinwiddie.

Daniel Morgan, 1736-1802 (Ch. 5), was a wagon driver in General Braddock's army along with his cousin, Daniel Boone. He was a witness to Braddock's defeat and learned the lesson well. During the American Revolution, he commanded troops in George Washington's Army. In 1780, he was given an independent command and fought the British at the Battle of Cowpens. Using open formations of militia and a battle line of regulars he soundly defeated a strong British force.

Israel Putnam, 1718-1790 (Ch. 7), joined the colonial forces in 1758 and witnessed General Abercrombie's defeat on the hill near Fort Ticonderoga. He then joined the rangers and was trained in open forest fighting. During the American Revolution, he commanded the defenders at the Battle of Bunker Hill where the British using linear tactics suffered terrible losses. He learned the lessons of history and served under George Washington to the end of the war.

Robert Rogers, 1731-1795 (Ch. 7-8), volunteered to form a company of rangers after Abercrombie's defeat. The rangers were trained for special operations and eventually several companies of rangers were used by the British in the war. One of the purposes of rangers is to raid behind enemy lines and fight psychological warfare. Rogers led a large raid in 1759 against the St. Francis Indian village near Montreal. Killing 200 enemy and destroying their village discouraged Indian help to the French. He also led the relief force to Fort Detroit in 1763 but the Indians did not engage him, perhaps because of his reputation. He was a captain in the British Army when the American Revolution broke out. He could have been a valuable asset to either side, but neither side trusted him. He did serve with the British in limited roles and moved to England after the war in 1783. Today, some of his training is still used by the United States Army Rangers.

John Stark, 1728-1822 (Ch. 7), was second in command of Rogers Rangers and knew the tactics of the ranger very well. In the American Revolution, he commanded New Hampshire troops and was in command at the Battle of Bennington in 1777. Here he used open tactics to defeat the Hessians that had moved into Vermont. His victory weakened Burgoyne's army that later surrendered at Saratoga.

George Washington, 1732-1799, (Ch. 3-5-7). It is only fitting that we end our story with the man we started with. In many ways Washington was a very lucky man. In 1753, he dodged an assassin's bullet and lived through a near drowning in an icy river. He used open tactics at Jumonville Glen but at Fort Necessity, he lined his men up in rows until he saw the folly in that. He survived the Battle of Monongahela with two horse killed under him and several bullet holes in his clothing. He was a wise council to both Braddock and Forbes, but his advice was not taken.

No one has ever challenged his bravery, even in the American Revolution he showed no fear. He knew the lessons of linear tactics even while trying to train regulars in the Continental Army. His two victories at Trenton (1776) and Princeton (1777) were accomplished with surprise and open tactics. He usually lost battles if he fought with linear tactics. Winning battles wasn't his strong point. It was keeping his army in the field to fight another day. He did this with his courage and honesty and that he had no personal goal. He refused any money or laurels during the revolution, staying with his troops through bad times and good. Even at Valley Forge (1778) he accepted the same hardships as his men. The principles of freedom and liberty meant more than vanity or wealth.

He started a war at Jumonville Glen and ended a war at Yorktown. It is ironic that his last battle of the revolution was fought with linear tactics. Like Quebec, the Battle of Yorktown was a European style affair. From a young 21-year-old officer in the forests of Pennsylvania, to a mature commander of the Continental Army at Yorktown, he knew enough about history to avoid the mistakes of history. No finer man could have been found to become the first president of the United States.

APPENDIX 1

FORT NECESSITY SURRENDER DOCUMENT

Please note: The word "assassination" emboldened by the author.

A. Articles of Capitulation

Capitulation granted by Mons. De Villier, captain of infantry and commander of his most Christian Majesty, to those English troops actually in the fort of Necessity which was built on the lands of the King's dominions July the 3rd, at eight o'clock at night, 1754.

As our intention has never been to trouble the peace and good harmony which reigns between the two friendly princes, but only to avenge the **assassination** which has been done on one of our officers, bearer of a summons, upon his party, as is also to hinder any establishment on the lands of the dominions of the king, my master; upon these considerations, we are willing to grant protection of favor, to all the English that are in said fort, upon the conditions hereafter mentioned.

1. We grant the English commander to retire with all his garrisons, to return peaceably into his own country, and we promise to hinder

his receiving any insult from the French, and to restrain as much as shall be in our power the Savages that are with us.

2. He shall be permitted to withdraw and take with him whatever belongs to them excepting the artillery, which we reserve to ourselves.

3. We grant them the honors of war; they shall come out with drums beating, and with a small piece of cannon, wishing to show by this means that we treat them as friends.

4. As soon as these Articles are signed by both parties they shall take down the English flag.

5. Tomorrow at daybreak a detachment of French shall receive the surrender of the garrison and take possession of the aforesaid fort.

6. Since the English have scarcely any horses or oxen left, they shall be allowed to hide their property, in order that they may return to seek for it after they have recovered their horses; for this purpose, they shall be permitted to leave such number of troops as guards as they think proper, under this condition that they give their word of honor that they will work on no establishment either in the surrounding country or beyond the Highlands during one year beginning from this day.

7. Since the English have in their power an officer and two cadets, and, in general, all the prisoners whom they took when they **assassinated** Sieur de Jumonville they now promise to send them with an escort to Fort Duquesne, situated on Belle River, and to secure the safety performance of this treaty article, as well as the treaty, Messrs. Jacob Van Braam and Robert Stobo, both captains shall be delivered to us as hostages until the arrival of our French and Canadians herein mentioned.

We on our part declare that we shall give an escort to send back in safety the two officers who promise us our French in two months and a half at the latest.

Made out in duplicate on one of the posts of our blockhouse the same day and year as before.

James Mackay

George Washington
Coulon de Villiers

APPENDIX 2

BATTLE CHART

Battle	E	/ C	E	/ C
Fort Necessity	350	100	700	20
Monongahela	1459	877	891	28
Early Morning Scout	3000	262	1500	282
Fort Wm. Henry	1400	400	10,000	nil
Ticonderoga	15,371	1944	3200	377
Quebec	4500	664	4500	1400
Bushy Run	460	115	900	125

British/American French/Indians

E= engaged
C= casualties (killed, wounded and missing)

This chart is provided for those interested in the actual number of combatants at the battles listed.

ANNOTATED BIBLIOGRAPHY

Alberts, Robert C. *A Charming Field For an Encounter.* Washington D.C.: Office of publications, National Park Service, U.S. Department of Interior, 1975. Excellent work including original sources on the Battle of Fort Necessity.

The Most Extraordinary Adventures of Major Robert Stobo. Boston: Houghton Mifflin Company, 1965. One of Washington's hostages spent much of the war behind the lines as a spy or prisoner. He had something to do with many of the people described in this book. A fascinating story.

Anderson, Niles. *The Battle of Bushy Run.* Harrisburg: Pennsylvania Historical and Museum Commission, 1975. A fascinating booklet found at the Fort Ligonier Museum. Original after-action reports of Henry Bouquet in this wonderful story.

Bird, Harrison. *Battle for a Continent.* New York: Oxford University Press, 1965. Very good on the entire war, easier to read than Parkman.

Downey, Fairfax. *Louisbourg: Key to a Continent* Englewood Cliffs, New Jersey: Prentice-Hall, Inc. 1965. Excellent history on Louisbourg from its beginning to its destruction.

Fortescue, The Hon. J. W. *A History of the British Army. Vol. II & III*. London: Macmillan and Co., Limited, 1899 & 1903. Many sources are now better with more research being done since these volumes were firs published. However, some of the major themes are worthy of consideration by the more advanced student.

Franklin, Benjamin. *The Autobiography of Benjamin Franklin*. Boston and New York: Houghton Mifflin Company, 1923. Franklin wrote this some 20 years after the events and some of the facts may be in error as much of the book was written from memory. Very interesting however.

Fuller, Colonel J.F.C., D.S.O. *British Light Infantry in the Eighteenth Century*. London: Hutchinson & Co., n.d. Published around 1925 this is one of the first works of a very talented military historian. Here is an in-depth study for the serious student.

Military History of the Western World. Vol 2. New York: Funk and Wagnalls Company, 1955. Excellent source to understand the development of the military and its relation to the events of history.

Goodnough, David. *Pontiac's War, 1763-1766*. New York: Franklin Watts, Inc., 1970. Gives a good general account of Indian relations after the French and Indian War.

Hertzberg, Hazel W. *The Great Tree and the Longhouse*. New York: Doubleday and Company, Inc., 1962. Very good source on Iroquois culture.

Kopperman, Paul E. *Braddock at the Monongahela*. Pittsburgh: University of Pittsburgh Press, 1977. The closest thing yet to a definitive study of the battle. This volume examines the letters of the survivors to establish fact from myth.

Mason, F. Van Wyck. *The Battle for Quebec.* Boston: Houghton Mifflin Company, 1965. A very good account of the 1759 campaign.

McCardell, Lee. *Ill-Starred General, Braddock of the Coldstream Guards.* Pittsburgh: University of Pittsburgh Press, 1958. A very scholarly biography of Braddock.

O'Meara, Walter. *Guns at the Forks.* Englewood Cliffs: New Jersey: Prentice-Hall Inc., 1965. Excellent on the history of Fort Duquesne. Well written.

Parkman, Francis. *A Half Century of Conflict, Vol. II.* Boston: Little Brown and Company, 1894. There are six parts in the series that although dated is still good reading.

Montcalm and Wolfe. 2 vols. Boston: Little Brown and Company, 1966. This volume is a must read even though it was first published in 1884. Parkman is still considered the authority on this subject.

Roberts, Kenneth. *Northwest Passage.* Garden City, New York: Doubleday and Company, Inc., 1936. Although a novel, this volume is excellent in describing the hardships of being a ranger.

Stacey, C.P. *Quebec, 1759 The Siege and the Battle.* Toronto: The Macmillan Company of Canada Limited, 1959. This is an excellent volume.

Weigley, Russell F. *History of the United States Army.* New York: The Macmillan Company, 1967. Shows the traditions of the U.S. Army beginning with the Colonial period and shows how American soldiers are a different sort of man than a European soldier.

ABOUT THE AUTHOR

Bruce R. Kindig is a retired teacher from the Davenport Community School district where he taught various history classes in his 39 years of teaching. He has a B.A. and M.A. degree in history from the University of Northern Iowa. *George Washington Starts a War* is his third book on historical subjects. His first book, *Courage and Devotion,* has received several book review awards. He also writes humor under the pen name of John H. Marsh.

www.ingramcontent.com/pod-product-compliance
Lightning Source LLC
LaVergne TN
LVHW092057060526
838201LV00047B/1436